STEAM
AROUND
PLYMOUTH

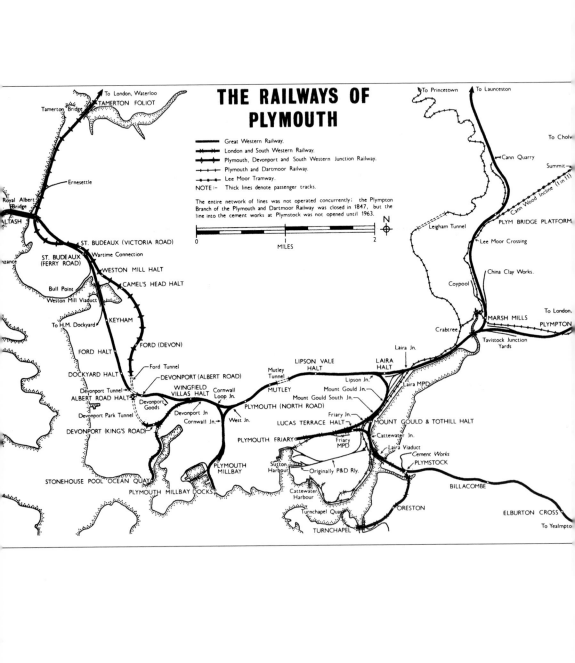

THE RAILWAYS OF PLYMOUTH

━━━━━━	Great Western Railway.
✕✕✕✕✕	London and South Western Railway.
━✦━✦━	Plymouth, Devonport and South Western Junction Railway.
┿┿┿┿┿	Plymouth and Dartmoor Railway.
●●●●●	Lee Moor Tramway.

NOTE :— Thick lines denote passenger tracks.

The entire network of lines was not operated concurrently; the Plympton Branch of the Plymouth and Dartmoor Railway was closed in 1847, but the line into the cement works at Plymstock was not opened until 1963.

```
0          1          2
        MILES
```

To London, Waterloo
Tamerton Bridge TAMERTON FOLIOT

Ernesettle

Royal Albert Bridge

ALTASH

ST. BUDEAUX (VICTORIA ROAD)
ST. BUDEAUX (FERRY ROAD)
Wartime Connection
WESTON MILL HALT
Bull Point CAMEL'S HEAD HALT
Weston Mill Viaduct
To H.M. Dockyard KEYHAM
FORD (DEVON)
FORD HALT
Ford Tunnel
DOCKYARD HALT
Ford Tunnel
DEVONPORT (ALBERT ROAD)
Devonport Tunnel WINGFIELD VILLAS HALT Cornwall Loop Jn.
ALBERT ROAD HALT
Devonport Park Tunnel Devonport Goods
DEVONPORT (KING'S ROAD) Devonport Jn.
Cornwall Jn. West Jn.

Mutley Tunnel
MUTLEY
PLYMOUTH (NORTH ROAD)
LUCAS TERRACE HALT
PLYMOUTH FRIARY Friary MPD

PLYMOUTH MILLBAY
Sutton Harbour
PLYMOUTH MILLBAY DOCKS Originally P&D Rly.

STONEHOUSE POOL "OCEAN QUAY"
Cattewater Harbour
Turnchapel Quay ORESTON
TURNCHAPEL

LIPSON VALE HALT
Lipson Jn.
Mount Gould Jn.
Mount Gould South Jn.
Friary Jn.
MOUNT GOULD & TOTHILL HALT
Cattewater Jn.
Laira Viaduct Cement Works
PLYMSTOCK
BILLACOMBE
ELBURTON CROSS
To Yealmpto...

LAIRA HALT
Laira Jn.
Laira MPD

To Princetown To Launceston
To Cholw...
Cann Quarry
Summit
Cann Wood Incline (1 in 11)
Leigham Tunnel
PLYM BRIDGE PLATFORM
Lee Moor Crossing
China Clay Works.
Coypool
Crabtree
MARSH MILLS
PLYMPTON
Tavistock Junction Yards
To London...

STEAM
AROUND
PLYMOUTH

Bernard Mills

TEMPUS

Nameplate of West Country class Bullied Pacific 34003 *Plymouth*, photograph taken at Plymouth, 19 December 1961.

To the volunteers who have built and operated
the Plym valley Railway

Front cover image: The London-bound 'Royal Duchy' passes through the cutting at Mutley on 16 August 1958. 4967 *Shirenewton Hall* pilots 6991 *Acton Burnell Hall*. Note the standard practice of placing the headboard on the inside locomotive, the leading engine would be detached at Newton Abbot after assisting over the South Devon banks.

First published 2003

Tempus Publishing Limited
The Mill, Brimscombe Port,
Stroud, Gloucestershire, GL5 2QG

© Bernard Mills, 2003

The right of Bernard Mills, to be identified as the Author
of this work has been asserted in accordance with the
Copyrights, Designs and Patents Act 1988.

British Library Cataloguing in Publication Data.
A catalogue record for this book is available from the British Library.

ISBN 0 7524 2814 4

Typesetting and origination by Tempus Publishing Limited
Printed in Great Britain by Midway Colour Print, Wiltshire

Contents

Acknowledgements

Many of the photographs have been supplied by my friends from the unofficial 'St Budeaux Railway Circle'. I owe a great debt to them, L.W. Crosier, M. Daly, M. Dart and T.W. Nicholls, who have not only allowed me long-term loans of their prints, but also much valuable information. If I have wrongly captioned any of their pictures, any error has been made in good faith. I would also like to thank all those who have allowed me to reproduce their photographs and I record all their names below with much gratitude. Where I have been unable to trace the original photographer, I have shown these as being part of my collection.

Author: 13, 25(t), 28(b), 35(b), 39(b), 51(b), 55(t), 56, 57, 69(t), 75(t), 88(t), 91(b), 97(b), 98(t), 99, 119(b), 126(b), 127, 128; *Author's Collection*: 10, 15(b), 24(t), 30(b), 31, 38(b), 41(b), 50(t), 50(b), 53, 54, 59(t), 61(b), 69(b), 71(b), 76(b), 82(b), 83, 88(b), 109(b); *The Late W.J.V. Anderson*: 49(b), 63(t); *D.H. Ballantyne*: 32(t), 117(b), 120(t); *H.C. Casserley*: 73(t), 79(b), 80(b); *R.T. Coxon*: 118(b); *L.W. Crosier*: 11(b), 12(b), 14(b), 16(t), 17(b), 21, 22(b), 33(b), 42(b), 44(b), 47(b), 57(b), 60(b), 63(b), 67(t), 71(t), 72(b), 75(b), 77(b), 79(t), 80(t), 94(b), 108, 109(t), 117(t), 121, 125, 126(t); *M. Daly*: 30(t), 33(t), 37(b), 43, 45(b), 46(t), 60(t), 79(t), 80(t), 89(t), 102(b), 110(b), 114,116, 120(b); *M. Dart*: 25(b), 28(t), 45(t), 48(b), 62(b), 64(t), 65(t), 65(b), 75(b), 86(t), 86(b), 87(b), 91(b), 97(t), 97(b), 49(t), 51(t), 59(b), 61(t), 62, 74(t), 84(t), 85(b), 95(b) 96(t) 104, 105, 111(b), 115(b); *M. Doherty*: 34(t); *P.W. Gray*: 16(b), 27(t), 36(b), 42(t), 119(t), 124; *I.R. Hocking*: 39(t), 40(b), 112, 113(b); *The Late R. Keene*: 11(t), 18(b), 19(b), 27(b), 98(b); *Mrs K.R. Mills*: 34(b); *T.W. Nicholls*: Cover, 14(b), 15(t), 17(t), 20(t), 22(t), 26, 28(b), 32(b), 36(t), 44(t), 46(b), 47(t), 48(t), 57(t), 65, 72(t), 77(t), 78(t), 85(t), 86, 87, 89(b), 90(t), 91(t), 92, 93, 94(t), 95(t) 96(b), 97(t), 100, 103(), 107(t), 111(t), 123; *The Late C.H.S. Owen*: 18(t), 37(t), 52, 55(b), 107(b); *C.R. Richardson*: 67(b), 68; *D.M. Rouse*: 20(b), 23(b); *The Late A.C. Roberts*: 81(b), 102(t); *The Late R.C. Sambourne*: 9, 12(t), 29(b), 35(t), 38(t), 41(t), 58, 70, 74(b), 110(t), 115(t), 118(t), 122; *The Late G. Treglown*: 40(t); *D.A. Thompson*: 113(t); *The Late W.L. Underhay*: 2, 23(t), 24(b), 76(t), 106; *A.J. Westington*: 81(t); *A.J. Westington Collection*: 101.

Much of the research has come from my own resources. I am indebted to: Arthur Westington for sharing his detailed knowledge of the workings on the former Southern Lines, and Friary Shed in particular; M. Doherty for his help with matters maritime; my fellow railway enthusiasts with their memories; B. Gibson for producing the map of the railways of Plymouth. Finally, may I thank Steve and Clare Fryer for their invaluable help typing the captions, John Lane for help with proof reading, Geoff Henderson for miscellaneous typing and my dear wife Audrey for allowing the living room to be taken over at times for the noble cause of *Steam Around Plymouth*.

To all who have helped me in any way, my grateful thanks.

Introduction

Steam Around Plymouth – an era which lasted for some 117 years from April 1848 to April 1965. It all began when a broad-gauge tank engine called *Pisces* arrived at Laira Green with the first test train from Totnes. The era concluded when another tank engine, a standard British Railways 80xxx, rather ignominiously dragged an ailing Warship class diesel into the city from Okehampton, on a very late-running train from Brighton.

The century and more which divides the exploits of these two humble tank engines saw the development, and contraction, of both the steam locomotive and the railways of Plymouth. In this book I have tried to recall some of the memories of those years. Much of the content is from the British Railways era, considered by many to be one of the most interesting phases of our nation's railway system. Having said that, I have been fortunate to be able to include sufficient material to take a look back to the Edwardian era.

In the heyday of steam, where the chocolate and cream of the Great Western mingled with the green of the Southern. To be fair, the GWR was the dominant player in Plymouth, the Southern having to take a lesser role. Take for example the engine sheds. The Great Western one at Laira was large, indeed the principal depot of the Newton Abbot Division. Just down the road at Friary, the Southern was a much smaller affair, typical of those scattered throughout the extremities of their system west of Exeter. Both are explored in this volume.

What then could be viewed on the rails in the Plymouth area? Well, the answer is plenty. Take for example the time I grew up (in Keyham) in the 1950s, when at exactly 12:45 by the Barracks Clock, on alternate weekdays 1010 *Country of Caernarvon* or 5098 *Clifford Castle* would dash past on the 'Up Cornishman'.

With atmospheric traction in mind, Brunel built the South Devon main line from Newton Abbot on the cheap. The resulting gradients left the Operating Department with a headache, which was not fully overcome until well into the diesel era. Expresses to and from the east were often heavy trains with substantial loads, thus invariably double heading with any combination of Swindon-built 4-6-0s was commonplace. For those which continued to and from Cornwall, Plymouth was an engine-changing point, although outside seasonal peaks, a single locomotive was normally sufficient.

In contrast, with the exception of the through Brighton service which brought the only restaurant car into Friary, the Southern expresses were two or three coach portions of trains which had emanated at Waterloo. For these the destinations in the more remote parts of North Devon and North Cornwall seemed to be of greater importance. A T9 on the Plymouth portion of the Atlantic Coast Express was a daily sight until about 1960. The Moguls, mostly of the N class, shared the other express duties with the Light Pacifics.

Semi-fast, stopping and local trains, both systems ran both. A two-coach all-stations to Newton Abbot or Exeter could have anything from a Castle downward and those to and from Cornwall either a Hall, Manor or Grange. Those to and from the Okehampton line saw the West Country/Battle of Britain Light Pacifics sharing the duties with the Moguls. Local trains to and from Tavistock North, Brentor (for the tea time train to get it out of the way of the Down Brighton) were in the hands of the M7 tanks. These were displaced towards the end of steam by the Ivatt tanks.

It is surprising that suburban services started so late after the railways had established themselves. The South Devon had reached the outskirts of the city at Laira in 1848, and the

City Centre at Millbay a year later. A further decade saw the Cornwall Railway open to Truro, yet by the turn of the century far more local traffic at Saltash crossed the Tamar by ferry rather than by traversing Brunel's masterpiece, the Royal Albert Bridge. In 1904, the great awakening came for the GWR which had taken over the South Devon in 1876, and the Cornwall (eventually) in 1889, but the advent of the motor bus saw the traffic eroded. It is a pity the suburban services enjoyed such a short heyday; the service to Plympton (and the Yealmpton Branch) ceased in 1930. Due to the lack of a road bridge across the Tamar, the Saltash service continued with an extensive timetable, the 64xx Pannier Tanks and their auto-trailers being replaced by diesel multiple units in June 1960, just sixteen months before the Tamar Road Bridge was opened.

Plymouth also saw a great variety of other trains – lengthy freights, a banker on the rear for Hemerdon. The Southern had its fast overnight London Nine Elms service in each direction, often worked by a Light Pacific. There were transfer freights between the yards, parcels and perishables, milk trains, indeed all manner of traffic now sadly lost by the railways. Let us not forget the Ocean Liner Specials from Millbay, a gleaming Castle with a schedule not far removed from that of the High Speed Trains of today. All are recalled within the pages of this book.

It was all worked by steam, by engines big and small. As 1960 dawned, great changes lay on the horizon. The combined effects of bus competition, car ownership, commercial lorries, line closures and dieselization were to have a huge impact on the railway system. In Plymouth the first diesels were shunters which arrived at Friary in 1957 to replace the B4s. The first main-line diesel was seen on the Western in 1958, but steam was still a common sight in Plymouth in 1961. In 1962 it still reigned supreme on the former Southern lines and the Western Launceston Branch, but by 1963 it was only used on the Southern lines in any quantity. Diesels finally took over the downgraded Southern (now Western worked) lines in September 1964. Within six months, working steam locomotives on the railways of Plymouth were nothing but a memory.

On 14 October 2001, ex-Falmouth Docks No.3, a little 0-4-0 tank engine, made history by becoming the first steam locomotive to power a timetabled train for some thirty-six years in Plymouth. This was the opening of the Plym Valley Railway (PVR), which has brought back a small stretch of the GWR Tavistock Branch. A new station has been built at Marsh Mills, and currently shuttle services operate for approximately half a mile to a point known as 'World's End'. Extension to Plym Bridge is well underway. Steam in and around Plymouth is alive and well; the PVR has a great future ahead of it.

I hope you, the reader, will enjoy this book. It does not set out to be a history of Plymouth's railways; that would be a substantial tome in its own right. They say the devil is in the detail. I have tried to include as much information as possible, and tell the story accordingly through the captions to the pictures, and to record for future generations what it was like, and what happened, when there was Steam Around Plymouth.

Bernard Mills
Buckland Monachorum
5 March 2003

One
The Great Western Main Line: Hemerdon to Saltash

The power and the glory – King 4-6-0 6023 *King Edward II* (now preserved) blasting through the woods midway up Hemerdon Bank, hauling the 08:00 Penzance to Paddington, 11:10 from Plymouth, 19 May 1954.

Plympton Station was situated at the foot of Hemerdon Bank. An Edwardian-era view looking east as passengers await the stopping train from Newton Abbot. Contrast this view with the picture opposite, taken some years later.

Steam Rail Motor services were introduced to the area in 1904. Train crew and station staff pose at Plympton as Steam Motor No.7 prepares to proceed to 'Saltash via Millbay'; the undated photograph is more than likely taken around that time. Regrettably, the heyday of the Plymouth area suburban services was short-lived, the service to Plympton being withdrawn in 1930.

The 6871 *Bourton Grange* pilots an unidentified King as they hurry past Plympton Station with the down 'Cornish Riviera' Express. A picture taken around 1958 before the station closed in March 1959. Contrast with the Edwardian view opposite.

For a time, some of the Britannia Pacifics enjoyed a sojourn based at Laira Shed, much to the dislike of the engine crews. One of these, 70017 *Arrow*, approaches Tavistock Junction with a down express in 19 July 1957. The picture is taken from Cott Hill Bridge.

The view from Cott Hill Bridge looking west on 10 May 1954 as an unidentified pair of 4-6-0s pass with an up express. Note to the right, the Pannier Tank busily shunting in Tavistock Junction 'Up' yard.

Cott Hill looking west again as 6009 *King Charles II*, unusually without a pilot locomotive, hurries past with the up 'Cornish Riviera' in July 1957.

The evening sun glints on 9F 92219 departing light engine from Tavistock Junction Yard to Laira Depot, having worked a freight from Hackney (Newton Abbot) on 25 July 1963.

1021 *County of Montgomery* heading the 06:25 Bristol Temple Meads to Plymouth, passing Tavistock Junction 22 May 1963.

This 1963 view is full of interest, seen from Lord Morley's Bridge which has since been superseded by the A38 Plympton bypass. To the left is the original Tavistock Junction Signal Box of the 1870s with the double-track curve that took the Tavistock and Launceston Branch round to Marsh Mills. 4992 *Crosby Hall* heads out of the Yard for Laira Depot, whilst a diesel shunter – a sign of things to come – shunts the 'Down' Yard. Tavistock Junction Marshalling Yard was extensive and was being used for overflow carriage stabling at this period.

The west-bound view from Lord Morley's bridge as 6025 *King Henry III* crosses the River Plym with the 16:10 Plymouth to Paddington on 18 February 1962. The scene to the right in the background has now changed considerably with the building of a supermarket.

Pannier Tank 4679 trundling along with a transfer of freight approaching Laira Junction on 4 July 1959. The railway at this time occupied a causeway.

The causeway at Laira is shown to full effect as Castle 7001 *Sir James Milne* passes with the 11:00 from Paddington on 31 May 1954. Regrettably, the reflection is no longer possible here as a dual carriageway road now occupies the site.

The Lee Moor Tramway used to cross the Western main line on the level at Laira Junction, the portion over the up and down main lines being removed on the night of 12-13 October 1960. Level crossing-type gates and signals controlled from Laira Junction Signal Box protected the tramway, which was boarded in since horses were used on this section. These features can still be seen as 6965 *Thirlestaine Hall* ambles past with the points set for Laira Shed. Viewed from Laira Junction Signal Box.

The Lee Moor Tramway crossing is shown to full effect as 6833 *Calcot Grange* and 6004 *King George III* approach with the 12:15 Plymouth to Paddington on 6 August 1959. Laira Junction Signal Box is to the left, behind which the former Laira Marshalling Yard has been dismantled and the site levelled to allow construction to start on the new Diesel Depot. Laira Steam Shed is in the background and two auto-trailers await the next duty in the former 'Up' sidings to the right.

Two years later the tramway has gone, the Diesel Depot is up and running and the up sidings to the right still contain a couple of auto-cars although use now includes track storage. 4985 *Allesley Hall* passes Laira Junction with the 12:40 Plymouth to Newton Abbot on 1 December 1962.

A historic view seen from Laira Junction Signal Box as 2832 passes by on the goods lines with a special train, conveying cables for the new Tamar Road Bridge then under construction in 1960. During a recent strengthening and enlargement of the road bridge not a single item was delivered by rail – how times have changed.

An almost Great Western view of the main line from Laira Shed as a Hall 4-6-0 4929 *Goytrey Hall* passes on a westbound goods service on 29 August 1948, just a few months after nationalization. The initials 'GW' and company monogram can be picked out on the tender; pure GWR signalling complements the view. The partial view of a loco coal wagon recalls that these were just as much part of any shed scene as the engines themselves.

With the former Lipson loops in the foreground, 4909 *Blakesley Hall* climbs the 1 in 77 gradient between Laira and Lipson Junctions with a down freight in the late 1950s. Milepost 244 ¼ (from Paddington via Bristol and Weston-super-Mare avoiding line) stands directly opposite Laira Shed on the remains of the up platform of the former Laira Halt, opened on 1 June 1904 and closed on 7 July 1930.

Light duties for a Castle as 5024 *Carew Castle* ambles pass the remains of the former Laira Halt with the Saturday's only 12:40 Plymouth to Newton Abbot. By this time (Spring 1961) Lipson Junction Signal Box, seen to the rear of the train, had been closed and its duties taken over by the Plymouth Panel on 26 November 1960, hence the appearance of colour light signals.

A busy, undated 1950s scene at Lipson Vale as 5078 *Beaufort* pilots another Castle on a west-to-North express. To the left on the down main line, a light engine heads from Laira Shed into Plymouth North Road Station.

Passing through the cutting at Mutley, the up 'Cornish Riviera' is seen leaving Plymouth on 12 September 1959 with 4955 *Plaspower Hall* piloting 6025 *King Henry III*. Note in the background a 9F simmering away in the holding sidings with the fine North Road East signal gantry straddling the mainline.

A favourite place to study locomotives awaiting their next turn of duty was the holding siding opposite the Royal Eye Infirmary. Seen on 18 February 1951, in the twilight of its life, is 'Star' Class 4-6-0 4023 *Danish Monarch*. Note the nameplates have already been removed as the engine was withdrawn shortly after the picture was taken.

Running into North Road past the Royal Eye Infirmary to the left, is 4300 Class 2-6-0 Mogul 7335 on a down goods in September 1960. Behind the third and fourth wagon of the train, an out-of-use colour light signal can be spotted beside the more familiar semaphore. This was just prior to the introduction of multiple-aspect signalling at Plymouth, one of the first power boxes on the Western Region.

Same day, same place. A 'sandwich' auto-train, formed unusually with three auto-vehicles instead of the normal four, trundles into Plymouth North Road with empty stock to form a rush-hour working to Saltash. The vantage point, a favourite for railway enthusiasts, is the Houndiscombe Road overbridge.

To save valuable occupation of the busy double-track section between North Road and Laira, light engines were often despatched to the depot in convoy. In this view from 14 June 1959, 6863 *Dolhywel Grange* heads 6845 *Paviland Grange* and 7820 *Dinmore Manor* with 6025 *King Henry III* bringing up the rear. North Road East Signal Box can be seen just beyond the *King*.

A view looking the other way at the station from the Houndiscombe Road overbridge, a fine panorama of Plymouth North Road when the signalling was still mechanical. In the spring of 1959, Hall class number 5972 *Olton Hall* carefully backs down to its waiting train on platform 7, with the Plymouth attachment to a Penzance to Paddington express.

On 11 March 1961, Castle Class 5075 *Wellington* (formerly *Devizes Castle*) arrives at Plymouth North Road with the 11:30 excursion from Exeter. It is conveying passengers for the county final rugby match played at Home Park, which was normally a venue for association football, being the ground of Plymouth Argyle. Unfortunately for the passengers, Gloucester won and Devon lost!

An undated but classic broadside view of a genuine Great Western King, 6016 *King Edward V* backing down to the Park Sidings, opposite platform 8. The photograph was taken shortly before nationalization, and incidentally the background is almost unchanged today.

Many a railway enthusiast has spent an hour or two in the back lane opposite the east end of North Road Station. From this favourite spot 'Britannia' 70022 *Tornado* arrives with an express from Paddington, date unknown other than pure 1950s nostalgia.

Castle contrast at Plymouth North Road. The 'North Road' suffix was dropped in September 1958, on the closure of Friary to passengers. The 5075 *Wellington* awaits departure with the return 17:15 Plymouth to Exeter rugby excursion on 11 March 1961. The present-day Inter City House tower block is under construction behind.

The 5051 *Earl Bathurst* and 4930 *Hagley Hall*. Coupled to a support coach, the pair await departure for Newton Abbot on 14 July 1985, prior to working an excursion as part of the Great Western 150th anniversary celebrations. Other than a diesel multiple unit bound for Gunnislake occupying platform 4 to the left, there is little to suggest that this photograph was taken some twenty-two years after the end of the Western steam era.

An intruder on the scene as the almost brand-new Britannia class Pacific 4-6-2 70021 *Morning Star* waits in the Park sidings with the Plymouth attachment for the 13:30 Penzance to Paddington (16:10 from Plymouth), in the summer of 1951. The Park sidings are still in use today, mainly for stabling Rail Express Systems van trains.

Whoops! Grange 4-6-0 6860 *Aberporth Grange* in disgrace at the east end of Platform 5 at North Road, having jumped the rails on 8 August 1959. The incident, although not serious, has attracted a good crowd of onlookers on Platform 7, whilst railway officials standing in front of the locomotive (not a yellow jacket in sight!) ponder how to rectify the situation.

Help is at hand as County class 4-6-0 1006 *County of Cornwall* is chained to 6860 for an attempt at rerailing.

The pride of Laira Shed, 5069 *Isambard Kingdom Brunel*, departs from North Road with the 05:30 Paddington to Penzance (13:00 from Plymouth), on 28 November 1959. The passengers travelling right through would have spent ten hours fifty-five minutes between Paddington and Penzance and stopped at forty intermediate stations, forty-one if it were a Tuesday!

In this 1957 view work is underway on the rebuilding of Plymouth North Road. The 6933 *Birtles Hall* awaits departure from Platform 6 with an express for Penzance.

The Old and the New (1). Gas turbine 18100 (left) on its first visit to the city on 4 March 1952, with 1006 *County of Cornwall* alongside. There is plenty of interest in this picture also. The railway official to the far left, standing on the boarded crossing, is the North Road Stationmaster, Mr G.H. Anthony, and behind him is the former Parcels Office, demolished to make way for the Panel Signal Box opened in 1960. The former North Road West Signal Box (closed November 1960) is to the right.

The Old and the New (2). 'N' class 31859 in February 1964, awaiting departure from Platform 2 with the 10:02 to Waterloo, the Plymouth portion of the up 'Atlantic Coast' Express. A 'Warship' class diesel has arrived at Platform 3, with the 06:25 from Bristol. Note the completed tower block behind, shown under construction on page 24.

A classic view of a Western Region named express. The 6012 *King Edward VI* on the up 'Royal Duchy' from Penzance to Paddington, seen on Platform 7 in 1957.

To relieve pressure on despatching engines to Laira for turning, there was a turntable at North Road West in the 'V' of the Millbay lines junctions. 2920 *St David*, the last of the class to be withdrawn, is seen on 18 August 1952. The site has been completely eradicated today. The turntable lasted from 1913 until removal in 1966.

Empty stock from Millbay to North Road for a Launceston branch working passes Cornwall Junction behind a 45xx Prairie Tank in 1960. The line to the right is the direct route from Millbay towards Saltash.

A fine period piece a portrait of the Edwardian era. Badminton class 4-4-0 3294 *Blenheim* at rest at Millbay Shed. The train crew proudly pose for the camera.

A northward view of the former Millbay (Harwell Street) sheds in the early 1900s. The line descending from Cornwall Junction to Millbay is to the right. Millbay Shed finally closed in 1931 when Laira was extended.

Millbay Shed, *c.*1905, with the saddle tank 1239 in between duties.

On 2 May 1959 the Railway Correspondence and Travel Society ran a 'Brunel Centenary' rail tour around Plymouth as part of the centenary celebrations of the Royal Albert Bridge. 6420 and its auto-cars are seen here on what was the approach to the former Millbay Station, the line to the docks is to the left. The new Pannier Market, opened in 1958, is behind the train. Note how dated the dress and appearance of the participants looks!

The 5028 *Llantillio Castle* climbs past Millbay Goods Depot (right) with an Ocean Liner Special to Paddington on 12 May 1959.

SR Mogul N class 31835 is a rare visitor to Millbay Docks, seen here on Millbay Road level crossing with a mixed van train bound for the Southern Region in the summer of 1958, the working due to extra traffic generated by a docks strike at Southampton. This particular scene has changed out of all recognition with no trace of the railway remaining, the Dock's cranes in the background are now also sadly only a memory.

Seen from West Hoe Road, an unidentified 1361 Class 0-6-0 Saddle Tank trundles along the East Quay past Jewson's Timber Yard, c.1958. At anchor behind is the Plymouth life boat. Dominating the background is a well-known city landmark, the grain silo, completed in 1943 and the only recognizable feature of this scene to survive. The West Wharf was transformed in the 1970s by the construction of the ferry terminal.

Sir Richard Grenville, the last tender to be withdrawn in 1963, is seen in that year alongside Millbay pier. With a speed of 13kt and able to accommodate 800 passengers, these giants of steam were a unique part of the GWR, a branch line from the sea.

Prior to the era of the jet airliner, a day could be saved on the eastbound journey from the New World by alighting at Plymouth for a Boat Train to London. Since Millbay Docks could not accommodate deepwater vessels, the liners dropped anchor in Plymouth Sound, passengers and mail being transferred to shore by tender. One of the latter, *Sir Richard Grenville*, is seen alongside the *Queen Mary* on her first visit to Plymouth in 1936.

Sir Francis Drake laid up alongside in the Inner Basin of Millbay Docks, with Jewson's Timber Yard behind, in 1954. Built in 1908, her career has now ended. Not long after this picture was taken, she was taken round to Marrowbone Slip in Sutton Harbour and broken up.

The GWR tenders were in fact mini-liners and are also fondly remembered for their local trips to the Eddystone Lighthouse, Salcombe and Looe. From the latter, passengers had the option to return by train. The penultimate Tender to be withdrawn, *Sir John Hawkins* is seen laid up in the Inner Basin of Millbay docks on 18 April 1962.

0-6-0 Saddle Tank, no.1361, is seen at Millbay Ocean Terminal in 1959. This was the pioneer member of this small class of locomotive introduced in 1910 specifically for dock shunting. The stock for a Boat Train to London has been berthed, the locomotive providing steam heat to warm up the saloons.

The RCTS Special described on page 32, viewed as it crosses Stonehouse Pool Viaduct, the original Cornwall Railway route out of Millbay. From 1859 to 1876 all trains had to reverse at Millbay until construction of the Cornwall Loop in 1876 (right) allowed for through running. This is almost from the same vantage point as the picture of the turntable on page 29.

At Devonport Junction the SR route to Waterloo (right) diverged from the Plymouth to Penzance mainline. The recently completed flats of Wingfield Villas form a backdrop to the westbound'Cornish Riviera'express with 6826 *Nannerth Grange* pounding up the grade, *c.*1958. This was also the site of the short-lived Wingfield Villa's Halt, 1904-1921.

Devonport is the longest-serving passenger station in Plymouth, having opened with the Cornwall Railway on 4 May 1859, predating North Road by eighteen years. In the autumn of 1960, Prairie tank 2-6-2 4549 is engaged on shunting duties. The mechanical signalling awaits replacement by the coloured light signal, marked with a cross, to be controlled from Plymouth Panel.

A busy, undated early 1950s scene at Devonport, the station known as 'Albert Road' under BR. Auto-coach No.126, formerly Steam Rail Motor No.59, brings up the rear of the 'sandwich' train from Saltash, left, whilst right, an unidentified 0-6-0 6400 class Pannier tank pauses with a train from Plymouth.

Emerging from the 117yd-long Devonport tunnel, an unidentified 'county' is seen from the former Devonport Station signal box, c.1949. The track work to the left looks somewhat complex for a small goods yard. Devonport Tunnel is unique in that the Southern's Ford Tunnel passes right beneath it; the crown of the SR tunnel is only 4ft beneath the base of the WR tunnel.

The Plymouth–Saltash suburban service only survived for so long because of the absence of a road bridge at Saltash until 1961. To accommodate the growing traffic in the Western suburbs, Dockyard Halt was opened in 1905 and is still extant. 6408 pushing towards Plymouth is seen as it pauses in 1960, just prior to its dieselization.

Right at the end of steam, 80000XX Class Standard Tank 2-6-4 80037 passes through Dockyard Halt with a green three-coach 14:15 Okehampton to Plymouth, in October 1964. The southern route from St Budeaux to Devonport had closed a month earlier.

Seen from the roof of the public convenience in Alexandra Park, an up express thunders past Keyham around 1955. To the left is the new Drake primary school, opened in 1954, and behind are the buildings of HMS *Drake* with the Barracks Clock Tower, a local landmark.

A busy scene looking towards Plymouth with Alexandra Park in the background. This is viewed from the footbridge at Keyham Station in the evening rush hour in April 1960. A four-coach 'Sandwich' train for Saltash, passes a three-coach one for Plymouth. In the yard, a newly introduced D63XX diesel waits with the goods from Devonport Dockyard.

Keyham Station opened on 1 July 1900 and is still extant. The Saltash rail-motor service was dieselised in June 1960. In the final weeks of steam operations, a 64XX pushes a standard, off-peak, two-coach formation from Saltash into the station, whilst passenger numbers grow for the next Saltash-bound service.

Plymouth was heavily bombed in the Second World War, the city paying a high price. On the night of 28-29 July 1941, Hall class 4-6-0 *Bowden Hall* 4911 received a direct hit at Keyham during an air raid. The houses in Johnston Terrace behind clearly pinpoint the location. The locomotive was withdrawn and not rebuilt.

Activity just to the west of Keyham at the junction with the line from Devonport Dockyard (far left). On 16 April 1960, 6400 is in the centre of a four-coach 'sandwich' for Saltash, whilst in the background D6318 & D6319 double-head the up 'Cornishman', then Penzance to Wolverhampton Low Level, over Weston Mill Viaduct.

The 6875 *Hindford Grange* is about to pass St Budeaux East Signal Box with a train from Penzance, c.1960. The photographer is standing in the short MOD-owned Bull Point Branch. Note the hoops on the signals from the Branch, denoting a non-passenger line.

A 'sandwich' train with the difference as a 64XX propels two auto-cars towards Saltash, with a couple of milk tanks on the rear. Seen from Cardinal Avenue, the double-track SR main line is in the foreground, with part of the SR sidings in the yard to the right, c.1960. The SR lines have since been obliterated. It was common practice to work empty milk tanks to Saltash in this manner.

Two views of trains at St Budeaux (East). 7813 *Freshford Manor* on a goods passes the Junction with the signals 'off' for the down main towards the Royal Albert Bridge, 3 October 1959. The left-hand arm is for the emergency wartime connection to the SR mainline.

Seen from St Budeaux (East), latterly Ferry Road signal box, County Class 4-6-0 1018 *County of Leicester* passes with the down 'Royal Duchy' from Paddington to Penzance, *c.*1958. The Bull Point Branch can be seen curving away on the far right.

After dieselization of the South Wales Valley Services at the end of the 1950s, some of the push-pull fitted 4575 Class 2-6-2 Tanks (so equipped in 1953) were despatched to the West Country. One of these, 5560, propels a Saltash bound train out of St Budeaux Ferry Road, c.1961. The station here was opened on the 1 June 1904 and is still extant.

The Main Line climbs at 1 in 62 from St Budeaux towards the Royal Albert Bridge. Passing the site of St Budeaux (West) Signal Box (closed 22 June 1952), and with the Down Loop in the foreground, 5915 *Trentham Hall* is hard at work in January 1953 with a goods train bound for Drump Lane, Redruth.

A closer view of St Budeaux (West) as 3100 Class 2-6-2 Tank 3187 ascends the bank with an assorted goods train. The date is unknown but certainly in the 1950s.

The single line over the Royal Albert Bridge was always a bottle-neck and, until 1962, was controlled by conventional single line token working. This was replaced by a King lever interlocking system which made for much more efficient working. 4950 *Patshull Hall* is about to give up the token, working the 'Up Milk' from Penzance to London, 3 October 1959. Photograph taken from Royal Albert Bridge Signal Box. The road bridge was not yet built.

Two views of Saltash-bound auto-trains with the fireman about to collect the single line token. 6410 on 3 October 1959 on a standard off-peak working. Control of the Bridge passed to the panel signal box at Plymouth on 2 July 1973 when the line back to St Budeaux was also singled.

Signalman J.D. Harris, a shareholder in the former GWR, looks on as 1434 propels towards Saltash in July 1957. Laira had two of this type on allocation for a while in the 1950s for working Tavistock services, one of which involved this working: the weekday 12:35 Plymouth to Saltash and 13:25 Saltash to Tavistock South, hence the engine facing Tavistock as per normal branch working.

The traditional goods train now seems such a distant memory. Such a working comes off the Royal Albert Bridge on 3 October 1959 with 7813 *Freshford Manor* on the front. Within two years the Tamar Suspension Road Bridge would dramatically change the view behind the train.

In a totally unique view from the Plymouth-end Tower on 26 May 1956, 6421 crosses the Devon land spans of the Royal Albert Bridge propelling an auto-train to Plymouth. The location was made possible as part of a PRC visit to the bridge. The NATO Naval Camp in the background has been swept away by the Tamar Road Bridge and associated car park on the site.

Right: Another different view made possible by the PRC visit on 26 May 1956. 6414 is seen inside the Devon span, under the great tubes with all the supporting ironwork. Regulations today would make such a visit almost impossible.

Below: The Saltash Corporation Ferry unloading its vehicles at Saltash Passage, with a substantial queue of pedestrians waiting to board, as an up goods crosses the Royal Albert Bridge in April 1951. The ferry ceased operation in October 1961 with the opening of the Tamar Road Bridge. The British Navy was a lot larger in 1951, with a good selection of the Reserve Fleet moored up in the River Tamar. The railway here is approximately 110ft above the river but that did not stop the mast of the Monitor Class Navy warship HMS *Roberts* striking the bridge in the early 1960s.

A brace of steam rail motors leave Saltash for Plymouth; a photograph taken in the Edwardian era, probably just after the introduction of the suburban service in 1904. The fare from Saltash to Millbay was then 6d (2½p in today's money). A day return from Saltash to Plymouth currently costs £2.10.

Fifty years later, the scene is little changed although the Royal Albert Bridge has been strengthened. A 64XX approaches with a train from Plymouth. Today's view would include the Tamar Road Bridge, whose opening gradually eroded the traffic; the last Plymouth-Saltash trains ran in April 1972.

At 07:00 on 16 March 1960, 28XX 2-8-0 Freight class No.3862 stands light engine beside Saltash signal box, patiently waiting for the line to be cleared over the Royal Albert Bridge.

A historic moment at Saltash as 1366 Class 0-6-0 No.1369 becomes the very last steam locomotive under British Rail to cross the Royal Albert Bridge on 20 February 1965, en route from Wadebridge to Totnes for preservation on what is now the South Devon Railway where the engine can still be seen at work.

Two
Special Occasions

A pair of ex-LSWR T9s was extremely rare, even more so on the WR main line. 30712 pilots 30726 as they ascend Hemerdon Bank near Stoggy Lane, with the 16:32 Plymouth to Exeter St Davids local service on 20 September 1958 (a train normally worked by SR locomotives and men). This was part of the daily exchange workings to keep the Western and Southern crews familiar with both routes to Exeter in case of emergency. The engines had worked an Ian Allan Special from North Devon; the return run to Exeter, also over the WR route, was by the equally rare sight of a 'Merchant Navy', see page 57.

Ex-LMS Coronation class 4-6-2 Pacific 46236 *City of Bradford*, seen from North Road West Signal Box in May 1948, having detached from the 13:30 from Paddington. The locomotive exchanges of 1948 brought some very rare and interesting visitors over the WR main line.

The exchanges were a first step towards locomotive standardization. Trials were run all over the country to examine the relative capacity and efficiency of most modern existing classes of each region. Royal Scot 4-6-0 46162 *Queen's Westminster Rifleman* again represents the LMS at North Road on the 08:30 to Paddington on 18 May 1948 – a pre-test run.

Amongst the ex-LNER representatives seen in 1948 was the fastest steam locomotive in the world, No.22 (soon to be renumbered by BR as 60022) A4 Class 4-6-2 Pacific *Mallard*, seen on platform 7 at North Road with the 08:30 to Paddington. The precise date is unknown but notice in particular the style of military uniform to the right!

With the Western Region Dynamometer Car (a coach fitted with instruments to examine locomotive performance) still attached, ex-SR Merchant Navy class 4-6-2 Pacific 35019 *French Line CGT* pauses in platform 6 at North Road, having worked the 13:30 from Paddington. A Pannier Tank has been attached to pilot the ensemble out to Laira. Precise date in 1948 unknown.

The GWR Legend 3440 *City of Truro*, the first locomotive anywhere to attain a speed of 100mph on rails in 1904, rests in Plymouth North Road at Platform 4 with the Westward Television Exhibition Train in April 1961. This special train toured the region to celebrate the launch of 'Westward Television', the first ITV station for the West Country.

The ex-GWR 28XX 2-8-0 freight engines were not a common sight on passenger duty. 2887 powers towards St Mary's Bridge, Plympton, with the PRC and RCTS 'Cornubian' railtour, returning from Penzance to Exeter on 3 May 1964. This was one of the last eastbound steam workings over the WR main line.

'The Cornubian' was the very last BR-operated steam train from Plymouth to Penzance and the first occasion that an ex-SR 'West Country' reached the far west. 34002 *Salisbury* waits at Plymouth for 2887 to bring the train in from Exeter on 3 May 1964. The Naval Chaplain arrived with minutes to spare to board the train for Penzance, announcing proudly 'that was the shortest sermon they will ever get!'

The 2887 has been attached at Plymouth for the return leg to Exeter, the new order in the form of a Warship diesel alongside in Platform 5 at Plymouth. The special headboards were made by the late Mr H. Liddle, the founder member of the PRC. 3 May 1964.

A rebuilt 'Merchant Navy' at Plymouth North Road. This was a rare sight as these locomotives were barred from working over the SR route to Plymouth. 35023 *Holland-Afrika Line* waits to take an Ian Allan Special over the WR route to Exeter, 20 September 1958.

The 'First Cornish New Potato Special' of 1958 from Long Rock (Penzance) to London hurries past Laira Junction with a County Class 4-6-0 in charge. The view taken from Laira Junction signal box, a busy Laira Steam Shed to the left.

Three
The Southern Main Line:
Tamerton to Friary

The Southern entered the city by way of the 117yd long viaduct over Tamerton Creek, the line to Devonport being constructed by the Plymouth, Devonport and South Western Junction Railway. Hauled by an unidentified T9, the 09:00 Waterloo to Plymouth Friary crosses the city boundary in this undated 1950s view.

An undated and anonymous gem at Ernesettle as a Southern Express, hauled by a 'Shorthorn' C8, runs along the banks of the Tamar towards Exeter, whilst behind, a GWR auto-train is seen crossing the Royal Albert Bridge. Probably photographed around 1920.

Seen from the Royal Albert Bridge on the occasion of the PRC visit on 26 May 1956, West Country 34038 *Lynton* is about to pass under the structure on a Friary-bound train. In the far distance, a freight train can be spotted in Ernesettle sidings.

A very unusual back-to-back formation to the west of St Budeaux, date and working unknown but early in the BR period. Still carrying its former Southern Railway number, 224, an '02' Class 4-4-0 leads another of the class, the already re-numbered 30183 fitted for motor train push-pull working. This is a Friary to Tavistock North local and 30183 would have been detached at Bere Alston for Callington Branch duties.

Originally 'St Budeaux for Saltash', renamed 'St Budeaux Victoria Road' by BR in September 1949, N Class 2-6-0 31837 passes through with a very mixed 07:30 Yeoford to Friary freight, the leading vehicle having come off the overnight Tavistock Mail. Photograph taken around 1960. The station is still extant, being served by the Gunnislake Branch Sprinter service.

The Western and Southern systems lay side-by-side at St Budeaux, but remained unconnected until a wartime emergency spur was installed on 20 March 1941, this being upgraded in 1964 to allow closure of the SR route to Devonport. BR Standard Class 5 4-6-0 No.73118 takes the spur with an Engineers' Special on 29 September 1964; the Southern Goods Shed is behind the train.

Although designed by the LMS, the Ivatt 2-6-2 Tanks proved very suitable for use in the West Country and BR built a batch for use by the Southern Region. One of these, 41317, prepares to leave St Budeaux Victoria Road for Friary on a local working from Tavistock North on 20 July 1957.

An extremely rare view of a passenger train taking the spur. GWR Moguls 6319 and 5339 double-head a Naval Leave Special from Keyham to Birmingham on 13 December 1953; the train diverted via the SR route due to clearance after a breakaway on Dainton Bank (between Totnes and Newton Abbot).

On the same day, 13 December 1953, ex-GWR 4300 *Calls* 2-6-0 Mogul 7316 approaches St Budeaux on the Southern main line with the up 'Cornish Riviera', again diverted due to the problems at Dainton.

'M7' Class 0-4-4 No.30036 approaches St Budeaux Victoria Road with a teatime Plymouth Friary to Tavistock North local train in April 1951. Note the former LSWR stock.

An unidentified 'Battle of Britain' Pacific crosses Wolseley Road Bridge with an up Southern Express. To the right the WR St Budeaux Ferry Road Signal Box and 250 milepost from Paddington. Today the signal box is a memory and the SR bridge and embankment have been swept away to allow for road improvements.

A view seen from the footbridge at Ford on 15 September 1963 as rebuilt 'West Country' 34108 *Wincanton* enters the station with an up train. From 1900 to 1947, a small goods yard existed here in the space just beyond the typical SR concrete platelayers' hut. Very little trace of this scene remains today.

Opposite: A panoramic photograph of Ford Station, taken from the inappropriately named Brunel Terrace. The 34010 *Sidmouth* rushes through with the Plymouth portion of the 'Atlantic Coast' Express in the spring of 1964. The line can be seen curving away over the 135yd-long Ford Viaduct to enter the 363yd-long Ford Tunnel. The Southern Railway at times designated this as Ford (Devon) to distinguish it from Ford (Sussex). The Plymouth to Brighton train ran non-stop through both!

Ford was partially built in a cutting and gave the impression of being more of a country rather than a suburban city station. 41317 arrives with the 17:09, Plymouth to Gunnislake, to pick up passengers on 6 June 1964.

On the last day of service, unrebuilt 'Battle of Britain' 34086 *219 Squadron* calls with the morning local service from Exeter Central, 6 September 1964.

There were two tunnels between Ford and Devonport Kings Road. Rebuilt 'West Country' 34095 *Brentor* emerges from the second of these, the 534yd Devonport Park Tunnel to pass the Technical College (top right) and enter Devonport Kings Road Station. The photograph was taken around 1962. Note also the lamp standard above the engine – it was originally a pole for the trams that once served Devonport.

Until the amalgamation of the Three Towns (Plymouth, Devonport and Stonehouse) in 1914, Devonport was a separate borough and the handsome LSWR station a fillip to the borough's civic pride. This is a view from the 16:52 Plymouth to Eastleigh hauled by Standard 5 No.73030 on the penultimate day of service, 5 September 1964.

From 1876 to 1890, Devonport LSW was a terminus, the arrival of the PD&SWJR from Lydford turning it into a through station. The suffix 'Kings Road' was added by BR in September 1949. 34080 *74 Squadron* prepares to depart with the 'Tavy Goods', the fast 17:21 Friary to Feltham and London Nine Elms freight service on 27 August 1964.

The 'Tavy Goods' again as the now preserved West Country 34023 *Blackmore Vale* brings the train under Paradise Road Bridge into Devonport Kings Road Station, 1 September 1964. No trace of the railway remains here; the College of Further Education has completely transformed the scene.

The view from Paradise Road Bridge looking East as an Ivatt tank arrives on the 17:09 Plymouth to Gunnislake service in June 1964. Devonport Kings Road handled substantial freight traffic; the wagons for attachment to the 'Tavy Goods' are ready and waiting.

An undated, late 1950s, view from the footbridge seen in the previous picture as T9 30712 approaches Devonport Kings Road with a Plymouth to Waterloo Express.

Cornwall Loop Junction as an unidentified T9 passes on a Plymouth to Waterloo train formed with a Maunsell set of coaches, photographed in the early 1950s.

By the end of the decade, the somewhat imposing telegraph pole has vanished to give a clear view of the Junction Signal for North Road (left) or Millbay (Cornwall Junction, right). Rebuilt Battle of Britain 34062 *17 Squadron* passes Cornwall Loop Junction 14 July 1959.

Southern trains joined Western metals at Devonport Junction (see page 37 top). The junction is just out of view to the rear of the train hauled by 34086 *219 Squadron*. This service is actually passing over the points at Cornwall Loop Junction to take the direct route into North Road Station. The double track in the foreground is the direct route from Cornwall into Millbay (see Page 36 bottom).

A three-coach train from Waterloo at North Road West, hauled by British Railways Standard 5 No.73030. The picture is undated but almost certainly is from the last few weeks of such trains operating in 1964.

The Western and the Southern side by side at North Road in the autumn of 1961 as the station tower block nears completion. The 6828 *Trellech Grange* is to the left, U1 Class 31901 to the right.

Plymouth North Road was a joint station between the GWR and LSWR (later SR), although the GWR owned the rails on either side, the LSW and SR enjoying running powers over GWR metals. Rebuilt 'West Country' 34024 *Tamar Valley* pauses in Platform 3 with a goods from Friary, *c*.1962.

Contrasts in the Southern-operated suburban services at North Road. These were not as prolific as those operated by the Western, but were important especially for the community in the Tamar Valley. O2 No.232 is departing for Friary around 1936 with LSWR 'gate stock'.

A similar view approximately twenty-five years later with the rebuilding of North Road almost completed. O2 30193 and Maunsell stock in BR livery have formed a train from Bere Alston, which will proceed, empty stock, to Friary for stabling. 11 March 1961.

Local services side by side at North Road on 5 August 1961. Left, M7 30036 awaits departure with the 17:27 to Tavistock North. To the right are the auto-cars of the 16:30 Tavistock South to Doublebois. How commuters of today stuck in traffic jams on the A386 would enjoy such a choice of services!

The LMS Fairburn 2-6-4 Tanks of 1945 were briefly seen on Southern metals in the West Country in the early 1950s, prior to the arrival of the Ivatt Tanks. 42103 was based locally for a while, seen here at Plymouth on a local from Tavistock North, c.1952.

Steam and diesel side-by-side early on the morning of 13 June 1964. BR Standard 5 No.73161 passes through Platform 7 at Plymouth with the overnight goods from Nine Elms to Friary. Hymek D7099 waits on Platform 6 with the 07:55 to Cardiff.

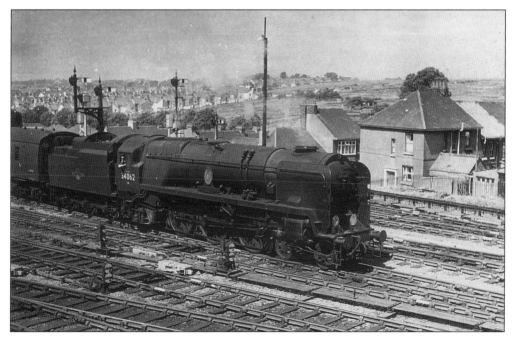

A view from the back lane as rebuilt Battle of Britain 34062 *17 Squadron* leaves North Road for Friary in the autumn of 1960. The GWR semaphores were replaced by colour lights in November 1960 when the panel signal box was commissioned.

The empty stock from Friary for the 13:18 Plymouth to Tavistock North comes under Houndiscombe Road Bridge behind Ivatt Tank 41316 on 27 February 1960.

30710 arriving on a Friary to Waterloo Express. The elegant lines of the former LSWR T9 are shown to good effect in yet another view from the back lane opposite North Road. Designed by Drummond and introduced in 1899, these 4-4-0s were capable of a fair speed and were nicknamed 'The Greyhounds'. The date of the picture is unknown but possibly sometime in the 1950s.

'N' Class 31845 on empty stock, from Friary, probably for the 16:00 to Waterloo (an N duty on a Saturday) passes the site of Mutley Station, opened on 1 August 1871 and closed on 2 March 1939 – it was only 600yd between Mutley and North Road stations.

Southern trains bound for Friary left the Western main line at Lipson Junction for the GWR-built curve to Mount Gould (known as Lipson No.1 Curve). With a busy Laira Shed behind, an N passes over the Junction for the 'Speedway' with an express for Friary in the late 1950s.

Having regained pure Southern metals at Friary Junction, unrebuilt 'West Country' 34030 *Watersmeet* passes Friary 'A' Signal Box with empty stock from North Road on 27 September 1958.

PLYMOUTH— Friary Yard.

A Southern Railway-era view of Friary Yard seen from Desborough Road on 14 June 1926. A rake of ancient rolling stock is stabled on the right, a 'T9' appears to be shunting and, in the foreground, the start of the walled cutting of the SR branch to North Quay. Tothill Road Bridge forms the background, Knighton Road is to the far right, with the spire of St Jude's Church behind.

A not too different viewpoint some thirty years later, in the BR era, as O2 No.30183 shunts the yard, unusually paired with a GWR 'match truck'. The North Quay line has gone (closed in 1950) and the passenger coaches have taken on a more modern look. Contrast with the picture on page 60 as 30183 has had its auto-gear (for working push-pull passenger trains) removed.

Also taken on 14 June 1926, the same day as the picture at bottom of previous page , a view of Friary Yard from Tothill Road Bridge showing the eastward view. Of particular interest are the Turner's fish boxes, to the right of the wagons, which have been unloaded and await collection by the fish merchant.

Looking from Knighton Road on to Friary Yard *c*.1952. B4 No.30088 fitted with a Drummond boiler (see in contrast page 115), acts as Yard Pilot. Note behind the walled cutting of the North Quay Branch, the wagons at the head of the Mileage Yard formed ready for the next trip to the Cattewater.

The London and South Western Railway's Plymouth Friary Terminus opened on 1 July 1891. Technically it became a junction station when the branch to Plymstock opened in September the following year. A busy Southern Railway era scene of 1926 with, behind Friary 'B' signal box, the Station Pilot left, a T9 ready to leave for Exeter, and to the right, an 'O2' on a Turnchapel Branch train.

'West Country' 34003 *Plymouth*, seen in this old photograph in its early BR livery at Friary, ready to depart with the inaugural British Railways 'Devon Belle' of 1948.

A Southern Railway period piece, T9 No.714 acting as Station Pilot at Friary on 22 May 1935. St Jude's Church stands proudly behind.

From almost the same viewpoint, some twenty or so years later (St Jude's Church top left). The BR era with M7 30036 on a '3 Lav' set of coaches waiting to form the 16:04 to Brentor. In front, a GWR Mogul waits to take the 14:35 stopping train to Exeter Central, this being one of the 'exchange turns' whereby the Western and Southern Region crews from both Plymouth and Exeter worked a daily turn over the alternative route to maintain full route knowledge in case of emergency. Friary 'B' Box is to the right.

Four
Laira – 'The Lair of Kings'

The Locomotive Depot at Laira opened in 1901 and was constructed to the GWR pattern of the time, being similar to Taunton (1896) and Croes Newydd, Wrexham (1902). Like the later, Laira was built in a triangle of lines, fitting in to the parcel of land enclosed by the main line, the Sutton Harbour Branch and the Lipson No.1 Curve. Much of the railway land at Laira had been reclaimed from the River Plym over the years, evident in this view of the Pioneer 'Star' Class No. 40 *North Star* seen here in its original form as built as an 'Atlantic' 4-4-2. The bare hillside beyond has since become the Efford housing estate, and changed beyond recognition. Exact date of the picture unknown but can be tied down to the period between 1906, when *North Star* was built, and November 1909 when rebuilt as a 4-6-0.

Many locomotive types were based at Laira over the years, ranging from the humble Dock Shunter to the mighty Kings. Here in the Summer of 1950, 1901 Class 0-6-0 Pannier Tank No.1990 is seen at rest. The class had been introduced as long ago as 1874.

The GWR was involved in a short-lived scheme after the Second World War to convert some locomotives to oil burning. Laira was one of the sheds involved and a fuelling point was established on the south side of the 'New' Shed. In this very rare view of oil burners at Laira, the temporarily renumbered 2-8-0 28xx No.4808 ex-2834 is seen in September 1947 with 4807 to the rear.

A splendid view of Laira coalstage on 11 February 1962 with County Class 4-6-0 No.1006 *County of Cornwall* to the left and Prairie 4575 Class 2-6-2 No.5532 to the right.

Although only a small class numerically, the light 44xx Class were a familiar scene at Laira for many years, the Depot maintaining a small allocation (until 1955) mostly for working the difficult line from Yelverton to Princetown. 4403 is seen at Laira in June 1951, having just been re-allocated from Wellington, Salop from duties on the Much Wenlock Branch.

Grange Class 4-60 6863 *Dolhywel Grange*, with large tender, at rest in the Shed Yard on 6 October 1954.

Laira Depot could undertake heavy maintenance, the Hoist being a most useful piece of equipment. King 6002 *King William IV* has been detached from its tender and raised for work on the front bogies, which have been removed for attention. Date unknown, *c.*1960.

Opposite: 6002 again 'on the Hoist', a powerful image of 89 tons of locomotive, held securely by the chains. Note the bogie, far left, has been removed for attention.

Right: The Hoist was also known as the Stationary Crane. Mogul 7325 is awaiting attention on 3 July 1963.

Below: I make no apologies for returning to the familiar view of engines by the Coaling Stage as there was always a variety of locomotives to be seen at this location. Not too common in this part of the world, '2251' Class 0-6-0 No.2230 is seen next to an unidentified 4-6-0, whilst a Pannier Tank is on coaling stage duties. Date unknown but probably late 1950s.

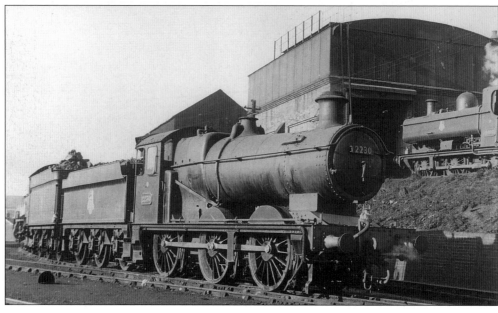

The need for coaling locomotives as they came on shed was forever ongoing, an engine being employed on coaling stage duties on a continual basis. More often than not one of the Pannier Tanks was used and 3686 is seen waiting to retrieve empty coal wagons on 22 November 1959.

A typical line-up at Laira, 4561, three unidentified Hall Class 4-6-0s, 5024 *Carew Castle*, 5065 *Newport Castle* and 1004 *County of Somerset*. The coaling stage is to the right. 22 April 1962. (4561 is now preserved on the West Somerset Railway.)

The same line-up as the previous picture, looking the other way towards the Roundhouse.

3849 and an unidentified 'Mogul' viewed from the coaling stage in 1962. Note the main line to the left, and in the background the Laira Junction Signal Box and the Embankment Road Bridge; it is from here that the pictures on pages 16 and 17 were taken.

A typical Laira Shed scene with 5024 *Carew Castle*, 5065 *Newport Castle* and 1004 *County of Somerset* on 22 April 1962. Although seen from a slightly different angle, the hillside behind has changed considerably in appearance since the picture of *North Star* on page 83.

Another engine which has been preserved locally, (at present undergoing an overhaul at Buckfastleigh, on the South Devon Railway) is 4920 *Dumbleton Hall*. It is seen here in the morning sunshine in 1963 outside the Long, or New Shed. An unidentified 4575 Class Prairie is to the right.

View this picture with the one opposite; together they present a complete panorama of the interior of the Roundhouse at Laira as seen on 15 April 1962. From the left: 1003 *County of Wilts*, 6988 *Swithland Hall*, Pannier 4658, Prairie 4555 (now preserved on the Torbay & Dartmouth Railway) and 6938 *Corndean Hall*.

The continuation of the picture opposite. Together they really convey the aura and atmosphere of Steam at rest. Again, from the left: Prairies 5564 and 5568, 5000 *Launceston Castle*, 4087 *Cardigan Castle*, Prairies 5541 and 5569.

The 6954 *Lotherton Hall* being coaled at Laira on 15 September 1963.

Incoming locomotives to Laira came on to the shed and were coaled, then serviced by the disposal men before going on shed. 2-8-0 3805 has been coaled and now waits for ash to be removed from the smokebox. This was dirty and unpleasant work and, it has to be said, some railway men were glad to see the back of it. Date unknown, probably 1960.

Laira will long be remembered for its thirty-five-year association with the mighty 'Kings', from 1927 to 1962. Here 6025 *King Henry III* is being prepared on 12 September 1959 for working the Up 'Cornish Riviera' Express; note the headboard already attached.

A stranger in the camp. LMS Ivatt 2-6-0 Mogul 46526 of Bristol St Phillips Marsh Shed being coaled and serviced in June 1952, having worked the fish train from Swindon. Behind is 6026 *King John*. Note the piles of ash from previous visitors to the coaling and servicing lines.

The Sunday Swindon Fish was always a good train for bringing new and rare visitors to Laira, indeed 75079 (now undergoing restoration on the Plym Valley Railway) first came to the city on this duty in 1956. Here, in what is thought to be March 1952, newly-built 2-6-0 Standard '3' 77006 rests at Laira after this duty. The locomotive was later sent to Scotland, being allocated to Hamilton Shed.

The Long or New Shed was opened in 1931. Built between the stores (also put up in 1931) and the Roundhouse, the Long Shed was straight with four lines. This was really the home of the main line 4-6-0s – almost being purpose-built. A general view looking west on 22 April 1962.

A classic line-up looking out from the Long Shed. From the left: 7909 *Heveningham Hall*, 6826 *Nannerth Grange*, 5014 *Goodrich Castle* and 6019 *King Henry V*. The new Diesel Depot can just be seen in the background. 11 March 1962.

After the closure of the former SR Shed at Friary in May 1963, the engines that worked to Plymouth over the route via Okehampton were serviced here. An unfamiliar type at Laira, as 'West Country Class' 4-6-2 34020 *Seaton* waits to return to Exeter on 6 June 1963.

With just an Ivatt tank for company, Standard '4' No.75022 simmers away with the Roundhouse behind. Photographed in June 1964, four months before Laira closed to steam, there is an almost eerie silence.

'The Speedway' was taken out of use on 11 August 1973 but reinstated in November 1979 as the direct route for all trains from Laira Junction to Mount Gould Junction. This allowed the former Sutton Harbour Branch to be absorbed by the new High Speed Train Depot. The south-westerly wind is still blowing strong to obscure the Diesel Depot on 14 July 1985 as 5051 *Earl Bathurst* and 4930 *Hagley Hall* await clearance to proceed. Notice to the left, the former Steam Shed is now used as carriage sidings. Compare also with the view of the 'N' on page 77.

Opposite below: The Speedway' was installed when the Long Shed was completed in 1931. It formed a new exit from the shed, being an extension of one of the depot sidings, to join the Lipson No.1 Curve at almost the halfway point between Lipson and Mount Gould Junction Signal Boxes. In this 1957 view, the last Castle to be built, 7037 *Swindon* leads an unidentified Hall with plenty of activity in the shed behind.

Five
Friary Shed

History has failed to record a precise opening date for the LSWR Shed at Friary. As far as I can ascertain, it came into use in 1898. This was a much smaller affair than Laira, consisting of one three-road shed with a hoist alongside, a small yard at each end and a not very large coaling stage. It passed into the control of the Western Region in February 1958 and was closed in May 1963. The shed, with the rear of 34023 *Blackmore Vale* (now preserved on the Bluebell Railway), and hoist with the breakdown train stabled beneath, are shown to good effect in this undated 1950s scene.

Still bearing its LSWR livery, T9 773 at Friary Shed in February 1924. The loco was built by Dobbs & Co for the 1901 Glasgow Exhibition and was re-numbered 733 in 1925 to make way for the 'King Arthur Class'. Of the people in the picture, the four in front of the loco are, from the right: H. Hurrell, C. Congdon and G. Tucker; all of whom retired as Engine drivers in the 1960s. The photographer's assistant has joined them with an Exeter-based fireman standing on the splasher.

The U1 Class 2-6-0s were not the most popular locomotives at Friary. The local crews nicknamed them 'Mongulliper', fast on the level, no good on the hills! 1900 in SR livery is seen on the turntable in 1937 – compare with 31901 in BR livery on page 72. Of interest to the right is the water tower that the local lads have scaled to use as a swimming pool. One wonders how such a practice would fare in the health and safety culture of today.

Broadside of M7 No.255 in the later Southern era on 30 August 1945. Note on the bottom right, the wooden wheelbarrows provided to transport hot ashes – this could only have happened on the railway!

The rather grandly named Plymouth, Devonport & South Western Junction Railway (PDSWJR) ran its own branch from Bere Alston to Callington and owned three locomotives for the purpose. One of these, *Lord St Levan* carrying its BR No.30758, is seen near the end of its life on Friary pilot duties in the mid-1950s.

The LSWR O2 Class came to the area in the mid-1890s and served until the early 1960s, being used on local trains to Tavistock, the intensive Turnchapel Motor Train Service (until 1951), Callington Branch duties from about 1929 and the Stonehouse Pool line. The engine-cleaning team takes a break beside 30183 on 2 May 1959.

The 'B4' Class 0-4-0 Tanks were introduced in 1891, primarily for dock shunting, and had a long association with Friary Shed until about 1957. Note the spark arresters fitted for working the Cattewater Branch. To the right, Driver Jack Ryder is oiling 30102 whilst the fireman checks the sandboxes prior to working either the 13:20 to Bayly's Wharf or the 14:25 to Cattewater. June 1957.

B4 30083 was the regular engine for the trip to Bayly's Wharf, a siding served off the Turnchapel Branch – seen here on the hoist road on 15 June 1957. The hoist, like the one at Laira, allowed engines to be lifted for attention to wheels and bogies. It was not an original feature of the shed, being transferred from Callington in the late 1920s after the Southern Railway had taken over the PDSWJR.

B4 30102 coupled to the 'Mutual Improvement Coach', a vehicle certainly of some considerable vintage. In this coach, men met in their own time to learn the Rules & Regulations, about their locomotives and how they worked, to improve driving tuition and other railway related matters. 19 October 1957.

O2 30183 fitted with auto-gear for working push-pull passenger trains on 16 April 1954. Compare this with the picture taken five years later on page 103 when the auto-gear had been removed.

'M7' 0-4-4 Tanks were another class with a long association with Friary Shed, normally being used for local services to Tavistock (North) and the 16:05 to Brentor in particular. One of the Friary trio, 30035, stands outside the shed, c.1960.

Six

The Great Western
Branch Lines

There were two GWR passenger branch lines originating in Plymouth, one to Launceston, the other to Yealmpton. Neither saw regular diesel operation. The Yealmpton Branch was an early casualty, succumbing to bus competition as early as 1930. It was re-opened (using Friary) from November 1941 to October 1947 to accommodate Plymouth people living in the country during the Second World War, and closed to goods traffic in February 1960. The Plymouth–Tavistock–Launceston Branch closed as 1962 ended and 1963 began. Ready to leave Plymouth (North Road) is 5541 with the 10:40 to Launceston on 11 March 1961.

Trains for Tavistock (South) and Launceston ran over the main line from Plymouth (North Road) for the three miles to Tavistock Junction where the Branch diverged from the main line. Only four weeks before closure, one coach is sufficient for the passengers as 6400 passes Laira Junction with the 12:45 Saturdays-only to Tavistock.

Looking the other way from the Embankment Road Bridge towards the scene pictured above, 6406 pushes the 16:30 from Tavistock South (to Doublebois) along the causeway with what appears to be a fairly well populated auto-coach, a goods van brings up the rear and 8719 is in the background. 16 May 1957.

A picture full of interest, taken from Lord Morley's Bridge (now superseded by the A38 Plympton by-pass) c.1962. A 45xx tank brings a train from Launceston around the double track curve from Marsh mills to join the main line at Tavistock Junction – the Marshalling Yard is to the right (see also page 14). Note on the left, the original South Devon Railway Signal Box.

Marsh Mills was the first station out from Plymouth on the Tavistock and Launceston Branch, which became single track from here onwards. Looking towards Tavistock Junction, the A38 road-bridge behind, 6400 pauses with an auto-train for Tavistock c.1962. Notice the width between the platforms, a relic of the era when the line was of Brunel's 7½ ft gauge. The new Marsh Mills, home of the Plym Valley Railway (PVR) is approximately a quarter of a mile north of here.

Right on the city boundary, 6400 pauses in Christmas-card conditions at Plym Bridge Platform, with the 12:45 Plymouth to Tavistock South. Note the wreath on the smokebox, for this is 29 December 1962, the last day of service.

An unknown working, but almost certainly the Inspection Special at Bull Point, terminus of the short freight-only line from St Budeaux East, GWR, at its opening in June 1916. Weston Mill viaduct can be spotted to the right of the train. This line closed in the late 1980s and, in one weekend during June 1991, the rails were transported to Marsh Mills for use on the PVR.

Not a normal scene at Friary as 1361 Class' 0-6-0 Saddle Tank 1363 pays a rare visit. It is now preserved by the Great Western Society at Didcot Shed. The train is a brake van special organised by the PRC on its way to Sutton Harbour – 3 June 1961.

The 2021 Class 0-6-0 Pannier Tank No.2097 approaches North Quay Branch Junction with a North Quay to Laira Freight, c.1954. Seen from the Cattedown Road Bridge, the Sutton Harbour Branch is to the left. This scene has been completely obliterated by road improvements, and is totally unrecognizable today.

The RCTS Special shown on page 32 at Friary prior to working over the Yealmpton Branch on 2 May 1959. 6420 is seen in the classic 'Sandwich' auto-train formation.

The Yealmpton Branch was re-opened to passengers for a few years during the Second World War, as described on page 106. It was fitting that the last train, a PRC Brake Van Special, thus ran from Friary. The 4549 waits to depart on 27 February 1960.

Later that day 4549 pauses at Plymstock, in the Yealmpton Branch platform. Plymstock Station was unique, being used by both the GWR and SR, yet it was physically remote from the rails of each company. A GWR train for Plymstock would have travelled over pure SR metals from Cattewater Junction. For the SR to reach the eastern side of the city, trains had to use pure GWR metals from Devonport Junction to Friary Junction.

Not a single yellow jacket in sight as 4549 calls at Billacombe Station with Colesdown Hill Bridge behind the train. The station building from here was donated to the PVR and it was removed stone by stone during 1989/90, and taken to the new Marsh Mills Steam Centre, where it is planned to rebuild it as an example of a classic late-Victorian era GWR station.

The 5412 was the regular engine for the 1940s service from Friary to Yealmpton, seen here in the last months of operation on 18 July 1947, at a very rural Elburton Cross Station looking towards Plymstock. The whole area has since been engulfed by housing development and the station here has been completely eradicated.

The above picture was taken from the bridge behind 4549 as she waits to leave for Yealmpton on 27 February 1960. At this time, Plymstock, Billacombe and Elburton were part of rural Devon, being absorbed, along with Plympton, by the city of Plymouth in the boundary extension of 1967.

Seven
The Southern Branch Lines

In appearance, a delightful Southern scene as 'G6' No.30162, the Friary Yard shunting engine, takes its brake van past Mount Gould Junction on the direct spur to Cattewater Junction, (actually pure GWR metals) to allow Yealmpton trains to bypass Friary, *c.*1952. On weekday afternoons, the Friary Shunter worked a freight to the GWR Laira Yard, thence ran direct to Cattewater as the move seen above. Also of note: the little train has just crossed the Lee Moor Tramway, easily identified by the infill between the rails.

There is little in this busy scene to suggest that Plymouth Friary had actually closed to passengers almost two years previously. 30193 waits to leave on a PRC outing on 14 May 1960, the brake van special surrounded by empty coaching stock. The station was used for these duties for some four years after the last passengers had alighted in September 1958.

Known as 'the income tax road', a reference to the almost unlimited overtime available, an additional siding was laid at Friary Shed during the Second World War. This extended to the rear of Lucas terrace Halt where B4 30088 is seen on 19 October 1957. Contrast with the picture of the same loco on page 80, it has since been fitted with an Adams boiler. Note also the fine bracket signal worked from Friary 'A' Signal Box for trains from Cattewater Junction.

Seen from Lucas Terrace Halt, 30088 again, approaching from Cattewater Junction in July 1957. The apparent single track to the left is the up main line to Friary Junction, the embankment hiding the down metals. There would also appear to be plenty of activity on the sports field in the Tothill Enclosure.

Opposite above: The Ivatt Tanks were not a common scene on the Cattewater Branch. Seen from Prince Rock playing Fields, an engineering train is seen crossing Embankment Road, possibly during work to replace the bridge, *c.*1962.

Opposite below: A classic SR Branch scene. '02' 30182 with ex-LSWR coaches S738S and S2622S wait at Plymstock for Turnchapel, forming part of the 'Brunel Centenary' tour on 2 May 1959. The connecting auto-train from Friary featured on page 111 can just be seen behind in the GWR platform.

Date unknown, certainly mid-1950s, as B4 30088 heads away bunker first from Plymstock, running light engine to Bayly's Wharf. The loco has just crossed Stamps Bridge, out of view to the right. Like so many others, this scene has been completely transformed by roadworks and is completely unrecognizable today.

A charming branch line scene at Oreston with proud mothers and prams of the time. Still carrying its Southern Railway number 182, the soon to be re-numbered 30182 on a Friary-Turnchapel working in May 1948.

The Turnchapel Branch reached its terminus by a rather impressive swing bridge over Hooe Lake. Regrettably, this was demolished in the autumn of 1963. 30182 and the RCTS Tour of 2 May 1959 traverse the structure – note the central span and the supports for when set for shipping. A rather more rural scene than that of today in the background.

The last train to Turnchapel was a PRC Brake Van Special from Friary on 30 September 1961, hauled by M7 30034; the class were rare visitors to the line. In the process of running around its train, the loco poses on the western end of the Hooe Lake Swing Bridge, the points are already set for it to run back into the station.

30182 and the special of 2 May 1959 at Turnchapel. Other than the 'RCTS' headboard and the people, there is little to suggest this is not the branch auto-train that had ceased some eight years previously. Even the 'Totem' station nameplates are still visible. There is no trace of the scene today the station has been levelled and the site incorporated into the Oil Tank Storage Depot.

N 31874 on the Plymouth portion of the up 'Atlantic Coast' Express, passing Stonehouse Pool Junction, Devonport Kings Road (c.1963). The third set of rails from the train form the start of the 1-mile 23yd Stonehouse Pool Branch, dropping away at 1 in 40. The line passed under the goods yard, the top of the tunnel just visible beyond the signal box (ahead of the loco just beyond Paradise Road Bridge).

Opposite below: Breakwater Hill is a fine vantage point for a very industrial Cattewater scene, *c.*1952. An unidentified 'B4' is pulling a train of oil tanks – hence the need for spark arrestors – out of the Esso Depot Siding. It is passing the old Plymouth Tar Works (demolished in 1971): the building with the chimney on the left is the old boiler house, note also the period road vehicles. Despite great changes both on and off the rails, the railway is extant here.

For most of its life, the Stonehouse Pool Branch was a freight backwater, being worked by the Devonport Kings Road pilot engine, always a Friary based O2. Here, 30207 is set to cross Richmond Walk, the original terminus for a while, on a short freight for Devonport. 20 August 1952.

The twenty-nine-chain extension of October 1885 brought the line to the water's edge at Stonehouse Pool. From 1904 to 1911, the LSWR competed with the GWR for the lucrative ocean traffic, establishing an Ocean Terminal, and running their own tenders into Plymouth Sound. Little trace of this activity – the only regular passenger traffic to use the branch – remains as O2 30193 pauses with a PRC Brake Van Special on 14 May 1960. The Royal William Yard can just be seen behind the train.

Eight
Industry and Preservation

Most of the industrial traffic in Plymouth was covered by the various branch lines and sidings, and thus worked by the GWR and SR, later BR. However there were a couple of industrial systems with their own steam motive power. One of these is the Marsh Mills China Clay Works, still working albeit with diesel power. Here, the fireless Bagnall Locomotive is seen on 14 October 1961, making one of its frequent visits to the Power Station to top up with steam. This locomotive is currently stored on the Bodmin & Wenford Railway, awaiting restoration.

Devonport Dockyard was, and still is, connected to the Main Line by a junction at Keyham (see page 42). There was also an extensive internal system connecting North and South Yards, complete with a passenger train service from about the late 1880s to May 1966. The Dockyard had a fairly large steam fleet, which finally finished in the 1960s. 0-4-0 Saddle Tank, No.18, pauses for the camera in North Yard on an RCTS visit, 26 January 1963.

The North to South Yard and return passenger service, despite its wooden coaches, offered no less than seven classes of accommodation (surely a world record?) depending on whether one was an admiral or a workman. No.18 is seen about to pick up its train at the Albert Gates stopping place, 27 March 1963.

By 1963, the internal passenger service was largely diesel-worked. However, to accommodate a PRC visit on 27 March 1963, No.18 was provided to work an afternoon service, seen here on arrival at the North Yard Terminus. Note the flat truck next to the engine provided for carrying toolboxes and other 'luggage'.

No.18 has run round its train and is now ready to leave for South Yard on 27 March 1963, providing a classic study of that rare sight, an industrial passenger train. Much of the North Yard system survives in freight use, and part has recently substantially been rebuilt for the needs of the modern Navy.

Built to the unique 'Dartmoor Gauge' of 4ft 6in, Lee Moor No.2 poses outside its shed at Torycombe (near Lee Moor) in June 1970. External restoration had just been completed by the Lee Moor Tramway Preservation Society (since absorbed by the PRC), prior to removal the following month to Saltram House, Plympton, for static display. Sadly, the locomotive was lost to Plymouth when it was relocated to the South Devon Railway at Buckfastleigh in the autumn of 2001.

Steam around Plymouth is alive and well in the form of the Plym Valley Railway. After a long and sometimes painful birth in February 1980, a small but very dedicated band of volunteers have laboured away to reinstate a small portion of the former GWR Tavistock Branch. Much heavy engineering in the late 1980s created Marsh Mills North Junction, seen here on 17 April 1995, with ex-Falmouth Docks No.3 running light engine.

Small is beautiful. An idyllic scene on the PVR in June 1995, as ex-Falmouth Docks No.3, the last working steam locomotive in South West England, trundles towards World's End with a demonstration freight. The engine was retired in 1986, arriving on the PVR soon afterwards.

Looking North from the new Marsh Mills Station in Summer 2002. The weeds have been swept away and the line brought up to the highest standard. Work is well advanced on the extension to Plym Bridge. The No.3 trundles down the bank with DMU, the latter running as coaching stock. The PVR will continue to grow, and preserve for future generations the sight and smell of the steam locomotive at work in the city of Plymouth.